Words Are Your Superpower

Unleashing Your Illuminating Gift

A gift to: _____

From: _____

Date: _____

By Dr. Kevin J. Fleming

Illustrated by Olivia Fregoso Medrano

Words Are Your Superpower: Unleashing Your Illuminating Gift
© 2022 by Dr. Kevin J. Fleming

Published by Grafo House Publishing
Guadalajara, Jalisco, Mexico / grafohouse.com
In association with Jaquith Creative
Bothell, Washington, USA / jaquithcreative.com

Written by Dr. Kevin J. Fleming
Illustrated by Olivia Fregoso

hardbound ISBN 978-1-949791-80-8
ebook ISBN 978-1-949791-79-2

Bulk discounts available for schools, public institutions, and events.
For more information or to contact the author, visit www.kevinjfleming.com

Printed in the United States of America
25 24 23 22   1 2 3 4

To educators, writers, artists, parents, speakers,
and learners everywhere.

Do you know that suspicion that you have huge unfulfilled potential?

It's that unrelenting sense that you are different. You know the feeling.

Deep down, something keeps telling you that you were made for more.

Well, you're right.
You are perfectly and wonderfully made.
And you are not "average."
In fact, you are exceptional.
And you have an unstoppable superpower.

You may be familiar with other superpowers:
Flight.
Strength.

Telepathy.
Speed.
But yours is even better.

Your warm and melodic tone
melts a person's anger.

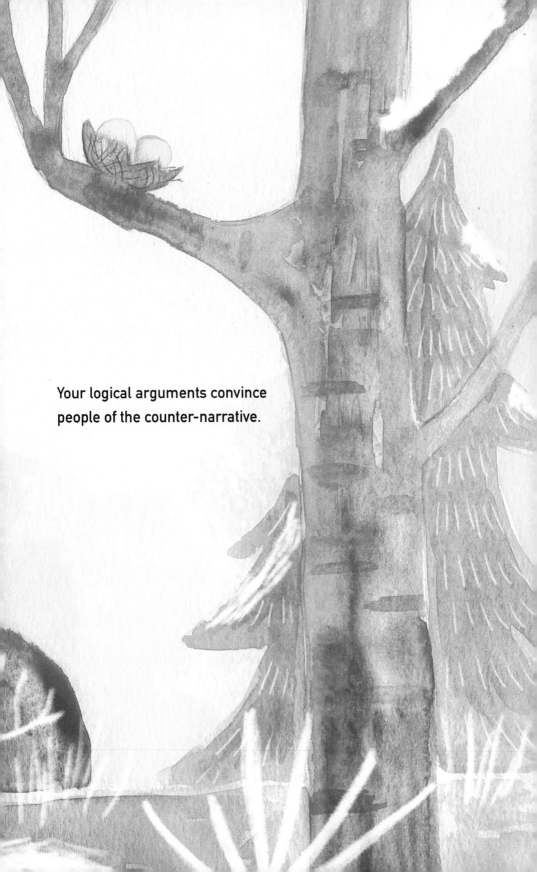

Your logical arguments convince people of the counter-narrative.

Your comedic prose incites deep laughter.
And a subtle suggestion emanating from your lips alters where people eat, who they date, and what careers they pursue.

It's true.

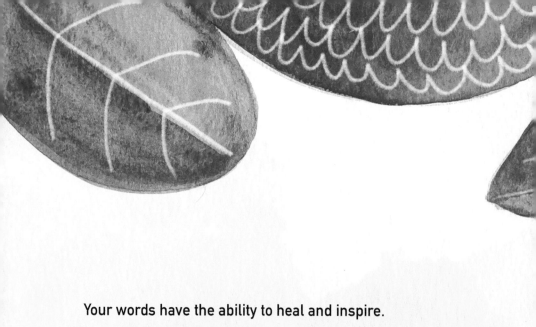

Your words have the ability to heal and inspire.
Your words have the power to pierce another's conscience.

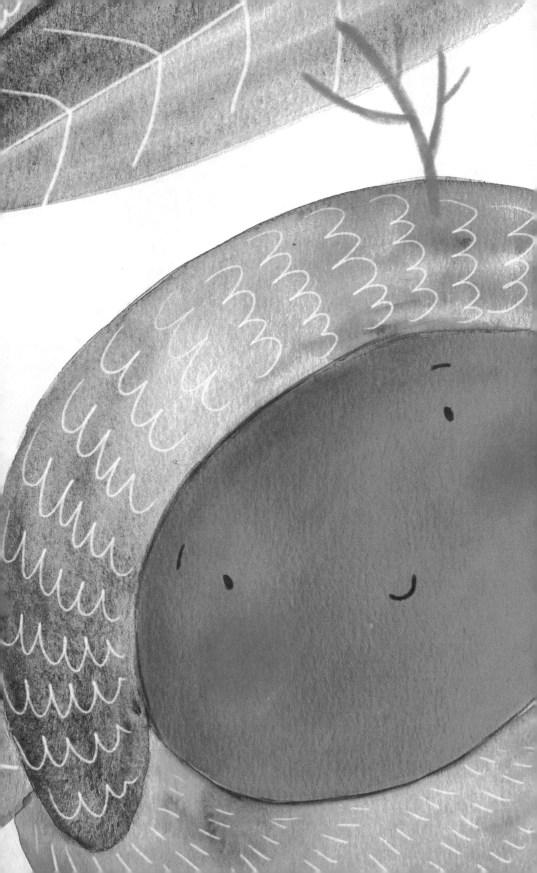

Your words destroy hatred and unify families.
Your words affirm self-identity, alter perspectives,
and influence the trajectory of people's lives.

What you speak and write
can influence change.

Your words destroy hatred and unify families.
Your words affirm self-identity, alter perspectives,
and influence the trajectory of people's lives.

What you speak and write
can influence change.

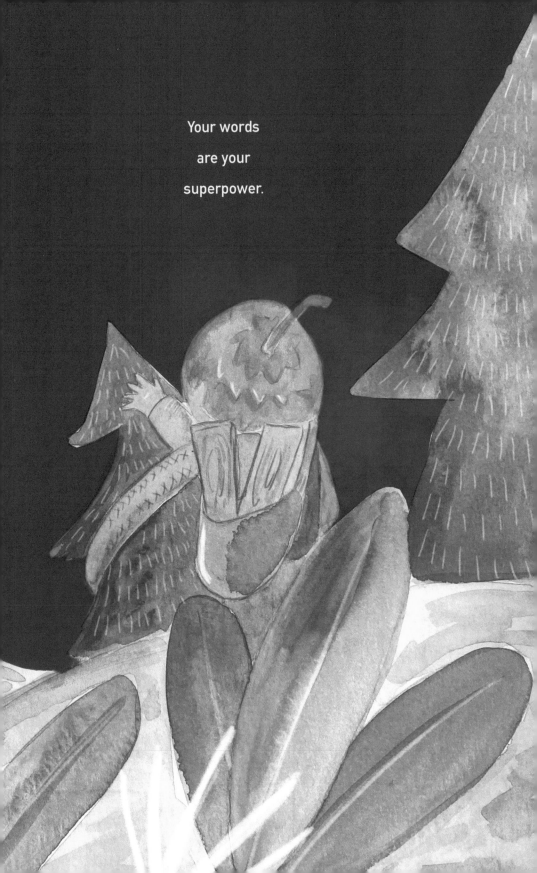

Your words
are your
superpower.

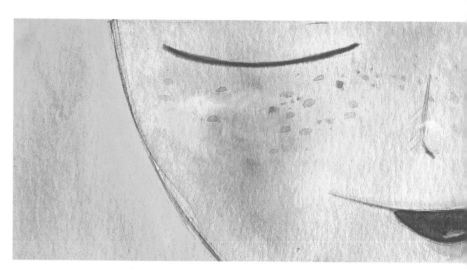

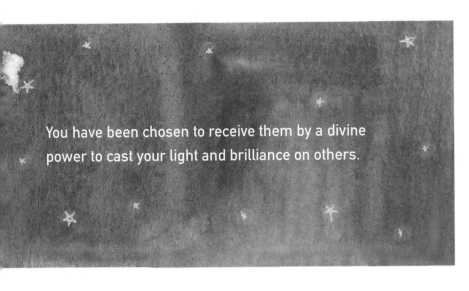

You have been chosen to receive them by a divine power to cast your light and brilliance on others.

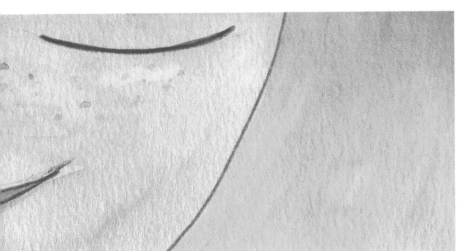

They are a gift to the world that you should not keep locked or hidden away.

Your intense words educate rooms, spark
movements, and launch revolutions.

Your important words become truth and forge
realities in the minds of all who hear you.

Your powerful words bond and sever,
shrink and elevate, shield and illuminate.

Your words manifest happiness.
They are kindling for the mind, capable of setting
fires in the heart and branding the soul.

Just as with all superpowers, this gift must be used responsibly.
Remove negative words from your vocabulary such as *can't,*
won't, and *shouldn't.*
Choose your words wisely and positively to encourage
and strengthen others.

Use your words purposefully to create a reality
around you that is good, and just, and kind.

Know also that the complete lack of your words – total silence –
is penetrating beyond measure.

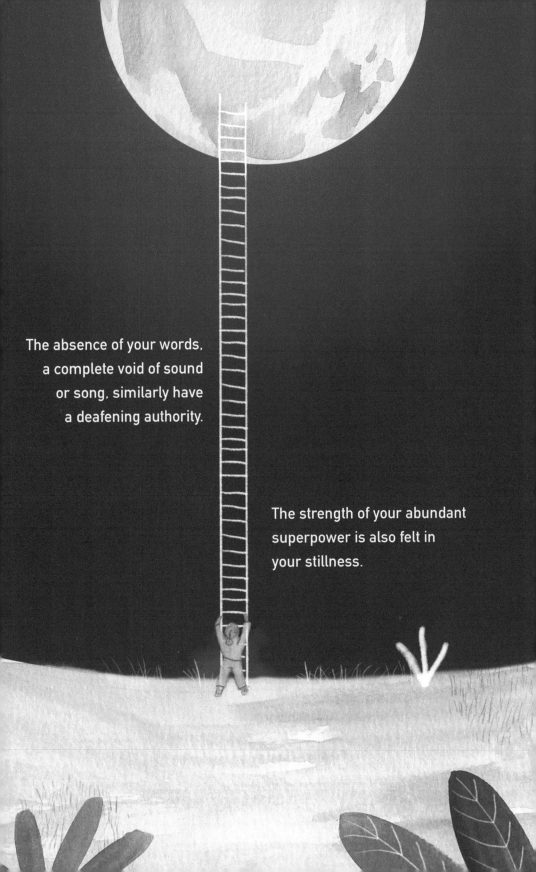

The absence of your words,
a complete void of sound
or song, similarly have
a deafening authority.

The strength of your abundant
superpower is also felt in
your stillness.

Your words not only can change the world,

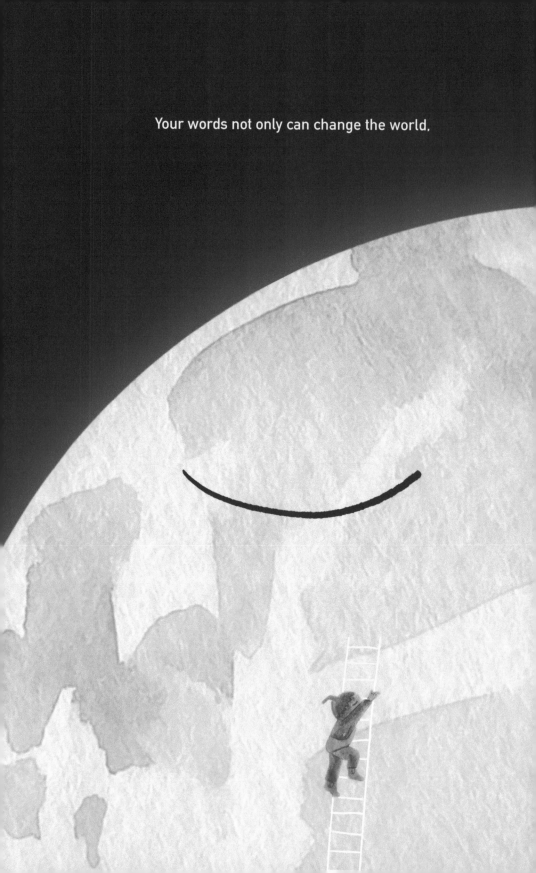

but they can create the future.
For others...

And for yourself.

About the Author

Dr. Kevin J. Fleming has witnessed the transformational power of language as an educator, Founder and CEO of Catapult, college administrator, and father. He is a passionate advocate for ensuring all learners intentionally equip their potential, enter the labor market with a competitive advantage, and find their purpose on purpose.

As President of Fleming Research International, his pioneering research inspires initiatives and awakens individuals across the globe. He is the producer of multiple viral animation videos including "Success in the New Economy" and author of several book titles, including the educational bestseller, *(Re)Defining the Goal* and the children's career exploration book, *There's A Hat For That!*

A philomath and recovering academic elitist, Dr. Fleming has earned five degrees studying in America, in Italy, and at Oxford University. He is a highly requested keynote speaker on the themes of career readiness, educational transformation, leadership, and language to a wide variety of governmental and professional groups. He is a proud eagle scout, member of Sigma Phi Epsilon Fraternity, and disciple of Christ. Dr. Fleming resides in California with his wife and daughter. He welcomes hearing from readers and may be reached through his website, www.kevinjfleming.com.

About the Illustrator

Olivia Fregoso is an illustrator and fine arts painter who has worked with clients from around the world for over two decades. Her extensive experience includes graphic design for newspapers and magazines in Mexico and Latin America, commissioned art pieces, custom design work, and book design, including several high-profile books that have been presented at the prestigious Feria Internacional de Libros (International Book Fair) in Guadalajara. She is currently building her company Olivia Fregoso ART / ILU. She has taught illustration and painting workshops for eight years.

Olivia's proudest accomplishment is her family: she is the mother of a fifteen-year-old daughter and twin 10-year-old sons. She is also an avid nature fan who enjoys hiking, ridings ATVs, and she is an animal lover and the proud pet parent to a Pomeranian, a cat, and a hedgehog.

Olivia received her degree in graphic design from the Universidad Autónoma de Guadalajara, with continuing studies in marketing and communications from the Instituto Tecnológico y de Estudios Superiores de Occidente. She also studied under the world-famous artist Gabriel Pacheco. Her art is known for its colorful, emotive qualities, innovative use of mixed media, and attention to detail. Follow Olivia online at www.instagram/oliviafregosoart and www.behance.net/oliviafregosomedrano.

Printed in the USA
CPSIA information can be obtained
at www.ICGtesting.com
LVHW070752260823
756256LV00013B/325/J